FOOTBALL'S GREATEST
RUNNING BACKS

Sports Illustrated KIDS

BY ERIC BRAUN

CAPSTONE PRESS
a capstone imprint

Sports Illustrated Kids Football's Greatest are published by Capstone Press,
1710 Roe Crest Drive, North Mankato, Minnesota 56003
www.capstonepub.com

Library of Congress Cataloging-in-Publication Data
Cataloging information on file with the Library of Congress
ISBN 978-1-4914-0759-2 (library binding)

Editorial Credits
Brenda Haugen, editor; Heidi Thompson, designer; Eric Gohl, media researcher;
Gene Bentdahl, production specialist

Photo Credits
Newscom: Cal Sport Media/Albert Pena, 14, 15, Icon SMI/Cliff Welch, 18r, Icon SMI/Mark LoMoglio,
19, ZUMA Press/Frank Mattia, 18l; Sports Illustrated: Al Tielemans, 5, 6t, 10t, 12r, 16bl, 17, 21l, 22l, 23, 25,
29, Bill Frakes, 11, Bob Rosato, 13, Damian Strohmeyer, cover, 6b, 9l, 9r, 24t, 26, 28, David E. Klutho, 10b,
12l, John Biever, 7, 8, 24b, John W. McDonough, 4, 16br, Simon Bruty, 16t, 20, 21r, 22r, 27l, 27r

Printed in China by Nordica
0414/CA21400595
032014   008095NORDF14

Table of Contents

*All statistics are through the 2013 season.

JAMAAL CHARLES

A 2012 game between the Kansas City Chiefs and the Oakland Raiders turned into the Jamaal Charles show. On the first drive of the game, he grabbed a short pass from quarterback Alex Smith. Charles avoided a defender just before the first-down marker and sprinted down the sideline for a 49-yard touchdown.

Charles was just getting started. He scored three more touchdowns before halftime and capped the day with a 71-yard touchdown on a deep pass from Smith in the third quarter. Charles finished the day with eight catches for 195 yards and five touchdowns. His performance helped the Chiefs to a 56-31 win and a spot in the playoffs.

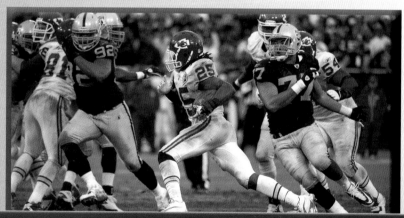

Year	Team	Games	Yards	Yds/Game	Yds/Carry	Rushing TDs
2008	KC	16	357	22.3	5.3	0
2009	KC	15	1,120	74.7	5.9	7
2010	KC	16	1,467	91.7	6.4	5
2011	KC	2	83	41.5	6.9	0
2012	KC	16	1,509	94.3	5.3	5
2013	KC	15	1,287	85.8	5.0	12

As a freshman at the University of Texas, Charles rushed for 11 touchdowns and helped his team win a national championship. The Chiefs took Charles in the third round of the 2008 NFL **draft**. But he didn't become the starting running back until midway through the 2009 season. In Week 17 he rushed 25 times for 259 yards, scoring two touchdowns and breaking the Chiefs' single-game rushing record. He was the NFL's second-leading rusher in 2010, but in the second week of 2011, he injured his knee. He missed the rest of the season but returned in 2012 to rush for 1,509 yards. In a 2012 game against the New Orleans Saints, Charles' 91-yard touchdown run turned the tide in the game and helped his Chiefs to a 27-24 overtime victory.

draft—the system by which NFL teams select new players

MATT FORTE

In a 2011 game against the Atlanta Falcons, the Chicago Bears had the ball near midfield. On first and 10, quarterback Jay Cutler dropped back and faked a handoff before tossing a short **screen pass** to Matt Forte. The pass rush had reached the backfield, giving Forte some room to run. He burst forward for 15 yards before a defender even reached him. One defender dove, and Forte stepped around him. He avoided more tacklers. One defender hit him in the shoulder pads, but Forte absorbed the hit and kept on running for 56 yards. Touchdown!

Forte grew up in Louisiana and played football for Tulane University in New Orleans, where he was the Senior Bowl **MVP**. The Bears chose Forte in the second round of the 2008 draft. He made an impact right away, rushing 23 times for 123 yards and scoring his first career touchdown on a 50-yard run. In 2011 he made the **Pro Bowl**, the first Chicago running back to do so in 20 years.

Forte is quick enough to make explosive plays and big enough to pound out the tough yards. In 2013 he rushed for a career-high nine touchdowns. He was rewarded with a second trip to the Pro Bowl.

Year	Team	Games	Yards	Yds/Game	Yds/Carry	Rushing TDs
2008	CHI	16	1,238	77.4	3.9	8
2009	CHI	16	929	58.1	3.6	4
2010	CHI	16	1,069	66.8	4.5	6
2011	CHI	12	997	83.1	4.9	3
2012	CHI	15	1,094	72.9	4.4	5
2013	CHI	16	1,339	83.7	4.6	9

screen pass—a pass to a running back or receiver who is protected by blockers at or behind the line of scrimmage

MVP—an award that goes to the best player in a game or a season; MVP stands for Most Valuable Player

Pro Bowl—the NFL's All-Star Game

ARIAN FOSTER

It was the last game of the 2010 season. Arian Foster was second in the league in rushing yardage, but he was having a good day. With the Houston Texans driving late in the game, quarterback Matt Schaub handed off to Foster, who ran through a hole in the middle of the line. As the Jacksonville defense closed in, he made a cut to the right and sprinted toward the open field. Three tacklers dove at him, and one clung to his hips as he crossed into the end zone for a touchdown. It was his second touchdown of the day and secured a Texans' win. It also gave Foster enough yards to claim the rushing title.

Year	Team	Games	Yards	Yds/Game	Yds/Carry	Rushing TDs
2009	HOU	6	257	42.8	4.8	3
2010	HOU	16	1,616	101.0	4.9	16
2011	HOU	13	1,224	94.2	4.4	10
2012	HOU	16	1,424	89.0	4.1	15
2013	HOU	8	542	67.8	4.5	1

Foster is one of the best running backs in the NFL, but no team drafted him out of college. The Texans signed Foster as a **free agent** in 2009 and gave him his first start late in the year against the New England Patriots. That day Foster carried the ball 20 times for 119 yards. Foster led the NFL in rushing yards in 2010. He also tallied 604 receiving yards and 18 total touchdowns. He led the NFL in rushing touchdowns that year, and he did it again in 2012. In 2013 Foster led his team with 542 rushing yards on 121 carries until a back injury ended his season.

free agent—a player who is free to sign with any team

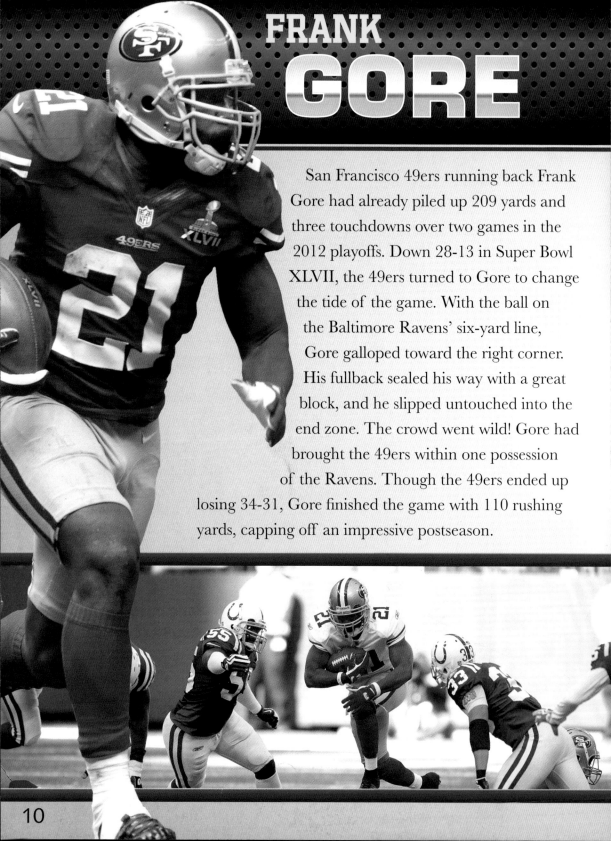

FRANK GORE

San Francisco 49ers running back Frank Gore had already piled up 209 yards and three touchdowns over two games in the 2012 playoffs. Down 28-13 in Super Bowl XLVII, the 49ers turned to Gore to change the tide of the game. With the ball on the Baltimore Ravens' six-yard line, Gore galloped toward the right corner. His fullback sealed his way with a great block, and he slipped untouched into the end zone. The crowd went wild! Gore had brought the 49ers within one possession of the Ravens. Though the 49ers ended up losing 34-31, Gore finished the game with 110 rushing yards, capping off an impressive postseason.

Year	Team	Games	Yards	Yds/Game	Yds/Carry	Rushing TDs
2005	SF	14	608	43.4	4.8	3
2006	SF	16	1,695	105.9	5.4	8
2007	SF	15	1,102	73.5	4.2	5
2008	SF	14	1,036	74.0	4.3	6
2009	SF	14	1,120	80.0	4.9	10
2010	SF	11	853	77.5	4.2	3
2011	SF	16	1,211	75.7	4.3	8
2012	SF	16	1,214	75.9	4.7	8
2013	SF	16	1,128	70.5	4.1	9

Frank Gore has been among the most dependable running backs in the NFL. Yet for most of his career, his skills had not been enough to build a playoff run. Then, in 2013 he and his 49ers played in one of the most dramatic Super Bowls ever.

Chosen by San Francisco in the third round out of the University of Miami in 2005, Gore hit the ground running in 2006—his first year as the starter. Since then he's enjoyed seven 1,000-yard seasons and five trips to the Pro Bowl. Gore is San Francisco's **franchise** leader in rushing yards and rushing touchdowns.

franchise—team

CHRIS JOHNSON

Under the bright lights of Monday Night Football in 2012, Chris Johnson and the Tennessee Titans faced off against the New York Jets. The Jets needed a win to keep their playoff hopes alive. Tennessee was backed up to its own end zone in the first half, and quarterback Jake Locker handed off to Johnson. The play was designed to be a punch up the middle—just a power run to get some breathing room. But Johnson found a hole and popped through it in a hurry. He was off to the races for a 94-yard touchdown. It still stands as the longest run in franchise history and led to a Titans victory.

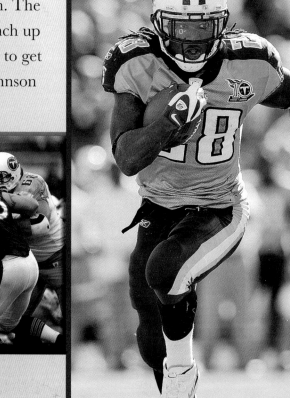

There aren't many NFL running backs with the big-play ability of Tennessee's Chris Johnson. He has the quickness to slip away from tackles and bounce out of clogged holes. He has the breakaway speed to leave defenses huffing for air while he flies downfield.

The Titans selected Johnson 24th overall out of East Carolina University in the 2008 NFL draft. A year later he won the NFL rushing title with more than 2,000 yards, just the seventh player to break that barrier. He was named the Offensive Player of the Year and has topped 1,000 yards rushing every season since he came into the NFL.

Year	Team	Games	Yards	Yds/Game	Yds/Carry	Rushing TDs
2008	TEN	15	1,228	81.9	4.9	9
2009	TEN	16	2,006	125.4	5.6	14
2010	TEN	16	1,364	85.3	4.3	11
2011	TEN	16	1,047	65.4	4.0	4
2012	TEN	16	1,243	77.7	4.5	6
2013	TEN	16	1,077	67.3	3.9	6

EDDIE LACY

The Dallas Cowboys hosted the Green Bay Packers in a 2013 matchup that both teams needed to win to help their playoff chances. The Cowboys had been ahead by as many as 23 points, but the Packers chipped away to pull within five points in the fourth quarter. The Packers got the ball back with 2:46 remaining in the game. Starting at the 50-yard line, the Packers relied heavily on **rookie** running back Eddie Lacy to move the ball up the field. He had already had a solid day, rushing for more than 100 yards on 16 carries. Finally, with the ball at the one-yard line, quarterback Matt Flynn handed the ball to Lacy, who leaped over a pile of defenders. Touchdown! The Green Bay Packers stunned the Cowboys with a 37-36 come-from-behind win.

In 2012 at the University of Alabama, Lacy racked up 1,322 rushing yards and 17 touchdowns. The next year he was chosen by the Green Bay Packers in the second round of the 2013 draft. A powerful runner who is also light on his feet, Lacy posted a stellar rookie season.

He ranked third in the NFL in rushing touchdowns with 11. He was named the 2013 NFL Offensive Rookie of the Year and was chosen for the Pro Bowl. Green Bay fans are excited to see what the young running back will do next.

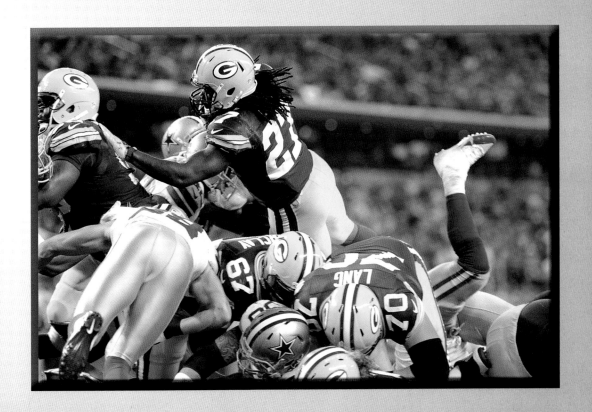

Year	Team	Games	Yards	Yds/Game	Yds/Carry	Rushing TDs
2013	GB	15	1,178	78.5	4.1	11

rookie—a first-year player

MARSHAWN LYNCH

The Seattle Seahawks led the New Orleans Saints 34-30 late in the fourth quarter of a 2011 playoff game. That's when Seahawks running back Marshawn Lynch went into "beast mode." He took a handoff, shook off a tackler, and crashed into the **secondary**. Then he shook off another tackle, then another. With one hand Lynch threw a defender to the ground. In all he broke nine tackles on his way to a 67-yard touchdown. Seattle held on to win.

Year	Team	Games	Yards	Yds/Game	Yds/Carry	Rushing TDs
2007	BUF	13	1,115	85.8	4.0	7
2008	BUF	15	1,036	69.1	4.1	8
2009	BUF	13	450	34.6	3.8	2
2010	BUF/SEA	16	737	46.1	3.6	6
2011	SEA	15	1,204	80.3	4.2	12
2012	SEA	16	1,590	99.4	5.0	11
2013	SEA	16	1,257	78.6	4.2	12

Lynch played football at the University of California, Berkeley and was the Pac-10 Offensive Player of the Year in 2006. The following spring the Buffalo Bills drafted Lynch 12th overall. The Bills made Lynch their starting running back for the 2007 season. He gained 1,500 yards in his first 19 games—a Bills record—and was named to his first Pro Bowl in 2008. In 2010 Lynch was traded to the Seahawks in a rare mid-season deal. Lynch finished each season from 2011 through 2013 with more than 1,200 yards rushing and also made the Pro Bowl each of those years. He also helped lead the Seahawks to their first championship in 2013.

secondary—the defensive players who are positioned behind the linebackers

DOUG MARTIN

The Tampa Bay Buccaneers were trailing the Oakland Raiders 10-7 heading into the second half of their 2012 matchup. Then Bucs running back Doug Martin took over. Early in the third quarter, Martin ran for a 45-yard touchdown to put Tampa Bay ahead. But Martin was just getting started. He added a 67-yard touchdown run in the third, then followed it with two more touchdowns in the fourth. Martin ran for a franchise-record 251 yards, leading the Bucs to a 42-32 victory.

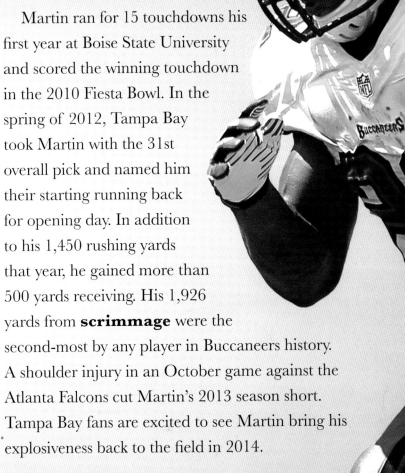

Martin ran for 15 touchdowns his first year at Boise State University and scored the winning touchdown in the 2010 Fiesta Bowl. In the spring of 2012, Tampa Bay took Martin with the 31st overall pick and named him their starting running back for opening day. In addition to his 1,450 rushing yards that year, he gained more than 500 yards receiving. His 1,926 yards from **scrimmage** were the second-most by any player in Buccaneers history. A shoulder injury in an October game against the Atlanta Falcons cut Martin's 2013 season short. Tampa Bay fans are excited to see Martin bring his explosiveness back to the field in 2014.

Year	Team	Games	Yards	Yds/Game	Yds/Carry	Rushing TDs
2012	TB	16	1,454	90.9	4.6	11
2013	TB	6	456	76.0	3.6	1

scrimmage—the imaginary line where a play begins

LESEAN McCOY

Trailing the New York Giants by one point late in the fourth quarter, the Eagles faced fourth-and-one in a 2010 game. Desperately needing a score, Philadelphia decided to go for it. Eagles quarterback Michael Vick bobbled the **snap** just half a second before pitching to running back LeSean McCoy. As Vick got clobbered by a rushing defender, McCoy squirted between two pursuers for a first down. Then McCoy turned on the turbo booster and rocketed downfield. The Eagles needed one yard so they could have a chance to score. Instead McCoy ran 50 yards for a touchdown and an Eagles victory.

Year	Team	Games	Yards	Yds/Game	Yds/Carry	Rushing TDs
2009	PHI	16	637	39.8	4.1	4
2010	PHI	15	1,080	72.0	5.2	7
2011	PHI	15	1,309	87.3	4.8	17
2012	PHI	12	840	70.0	4.2	2
2013	PHI	16	1,607	100.4	5.1	9

Philadelphia drafted McCoy out of the University of Pittsburgh in the second round in 2009. He became the team's starting running back for the 2010 season, during which he rushed for more than 1,000 yards and seven touchdowns. In 2011 he was the league's fourth leading rusher, even though he sat out the last game of the year.

McCoy led the league with 17 rushing touchdowns that year and caught three touchdown passes—becoming the Eagles' record holder for most touchdowns in a season. In 2013 McCoy led the league in rushing with 1,607 yards and earned his second appearance in the Pro Bowl.

snap—the act of the center putting the football in play from the line of scrimmage

ALFRED MORRIS

The last game of the 2012 regular season was a good one for Washington Redskins running back Alfred Morris. The rookie had already scored two touchdowns against the Dallas Cowboys that game, and his team was lining up on the one-yard line. The handoff came to Morris, and he hit the line hard. Dallas expected the play and closed it off perfectly. But Morris kept pushing the pile, cranking his legs until he thrust himself into the end zone. Touchdown! Behind Morris' amazing play, the Redskins earned a 28-18 victory.

Year	Team	Games	Yards	Yds/Game	Yds/Carry	Rushing TDs
2012	WSH	16	1,613	100.8	4.8	13
2013	WSH	16	1,275	79.7	4.6	7

Morris was just 72 yards short of becoming the first Florida Atlantic University player to have back-to-back 1,000-yard seasons. The Washington Redskins saw his potential and chose him in the sixth round of the 2012 draft. Morris quickly got noticed. He outshined veteran Tim Hightower in training camp to become the team's starting running back. He carried the ball 28 times on opening day for 96 yards and two touchdowns. He was named NFL Rookie of the Week three times. His 200 yards and three touchdowns in the final week against Dallas put his team in the playoffs for the first time since 2007. In 2013 Morris was named to his first Pro Bowl.

ADRIAN PETERSON

The Minnesota Vikings went into their last game of the 2012 season needing a win to get into the playoffs. Running back Adrian Peterson had to have a big day, and he delivered. He carried the ball 34 times for 199 yards and two touchdowns. With only seconds left in the fourth quarter and the score knotted at 34, Minnesota turned to Peterson again.

He took a handoff and barreled around the left end, breaking through Green Bay's defensive line. It took two Packers to bring Peterson down, but not until he'd picked up 26 yards to set up the game-winning field goal.

Year	Team	Games	Yards	Yds/Game	Yds/Carry	Rushing TDs
2007	MIN	14	1,341	95.8	5.6	12
2008	MIN	16	1,760	110.0	4.8	10
2009	MIN	16	1,383	86.4	4.4	18
2010	MIN	15	1,298	86.5	4.6	12
2011	MIN	12	970	80.8	4.7	12
2012	MIN	16	2,097	131.1	6.0	12
2013	MIN	14	1,266	90.4	4.5	10

Peterson is already one of the best backs in NFL history—and he's not done yet. His power, speed, and **agility** form a rare combination that put him among the best of all time.

Peterson played college ball at the University of Oklahoma and was drafted seventh overall by the Vikings in 2007. In his fifth game, he blew up for 224 yards as a backup. He was named the 2007 NFL Offensive Rookie of the Year. He had strong seasons the following three years, but his 2011 season came to an end when he tore up his left knee. Doctors said Peterson would miss at least half of the 2012 season, but he played all 16 games and led his team to the playoffs. He even came within eight yards of breaking Eric Dickerson's all-time single-season rushing record and was named the 2012 MVP.

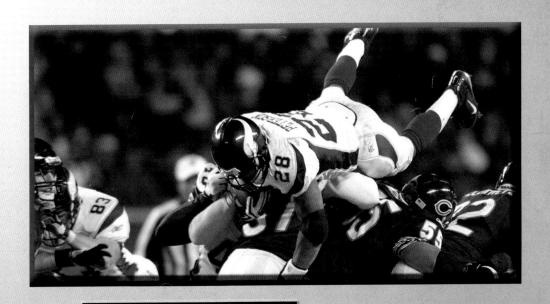

agility—the ability to move fast and easily

Less than two minutes remained in the 2012 game against the San Diego Chargers, and the Baltimore Ravens trailed by three points. They faced an almost impossible situation: fourth and 29. Desperate for a big play, quarterback Joe Flacco dropped back and looked downfield. But no receiver was open. That's when he found Ray Rice for a dump-off pass. Rice turned upfield and burst through the defenders. Breaking tackle after tackle, he turned the short pass into a gain of 29 yards and a few inches—just enough for a first down! His team tied the game on a field goal and won it in overtime. It was a big step on the road to a Super Bowl victory later that season.

Year	Team	Games	Yards	Yds/Game	Yds/Carry	Rushing TDs
2008	BAL	13	454	34.9	4.2	0
2009	BAL	16	1,339	83.7	5.3	7
2010	BAL	16	1,220	76.3	4.0	5
2011	BAL	16	1,364	85.3	4.7	12
2012	BAL	16	1,143	71.4	4.4	9
2013	BAL	15	660	44.0	3.1	4

Drafted out of Rutgers University in the second round in 2008, Rice became the Ravens' starting running back in 2009. Rice erupted for more than 1,300 yards and seven touchdowns, adding an 83-yard run against New England in a playoff victory. Rice emerged in 2010 as a big-time runner and a great receiver. In 2011 he scored 16 touchdowns—12 rushing and four receiving—and even added one passing touchdown. The 2012 season was an amazing journey for Rice and the Ravens, one that ended with a championship. Rice's 12-yard run in the fourth quarter of the Super Bowl helped keep the game-winning drive alive as the Ravens held on for a 34-29 victory.

C.J. SPILLER

In a December 2012 game against the Jacksonville Jaguars, the Buffalo Bills were driving in the fourth quarter. Running back C.J. Spiller started a run on the right side, but the Jaguars were expecting it. They clogged up Spiller's running lane and seemed to have him trapped. But instead of being tackled for a loss, Spiller sidestepped out of the hole. He danced around the left end of the line and charged 44 yards for the touchdown.

Year	Team	Games	Yards	Yds/Game	Yds/Carry	Rushing TDs
2010	BUF	14	283	20.2	3.8	0
2011	BUF	16	561	35.1	5.2	4
2012	BUF	16	1,244	77.8	6.0	6
2013	BUF	15	933	62.2	4.6	2

Elusive and quick, Spiller might be the most slippery ball carrier in the NFL. He excels at getting yards after contact and slipping past defenders. It's no wonder his nickname is Thriller!

The Bills drafted Spiller with the ninth overall pick of the 2010 draft out of Clemson. He didn't get much action that year as a backup to Fred Jackson, but in 2012, Spiller really got a chance to show what he is made of. He chalked up 207 rushes for a season total of 1,244 yards. He rushed for six touchdowns and added two more receiving. Spiller's breakout year earned him a spot in the 2012 Pro Bowl.

Glossary

agility—the ability to move fast and easily

draft—the system by which NFL teams select new players

franchise—team

free agent—a player who is free to sign with any team

MVP—an award that goes to the best player in a game or a season; MVP stands for Most Valuable Player

Pro Bowl—the NFL's All-Star Game

rookie—a first-year player

secondary—the defensive players who are positioned behind the linebackers

screen pass—a pass to a running back or receiver who is protected by blockers at or behind the line of scrimmage

scrimmage—the imaginary line where a play begins

snap—the act of the center putting the football in play from the line of scrimmage

Read More

Der, Bob, ed. *Sports Illustrated Kids Big Book of Who Football*. New York: Time Home Entertainment Inc., 2013.

Doeden, Matt. *The World's Greatest Football Players*. Sports Illustrated Kids. Mankato, Minn.: Capstone Press, 2010.

Scheff, Matt. *The Best NFL Running Backs of All Time*. NFL's Best Ever. Minneapolis: ABDO Pub. Co., 2013.

Internet Sites

FactHound offers a safe, fun way to find Internet sites related to this book. All of the sites on FactHound have been researched by our staff.

Here's all you do:

Visit *www.facthound.com*

Type in this code: 9781491407592

Super-cool stuff!

Check out projects, games and lots more at
www.capstonekids.com